my first years
journal for girls

images by
ANNE GEDDES

this special book belongs to

_____

with love from

_____

contents

contents

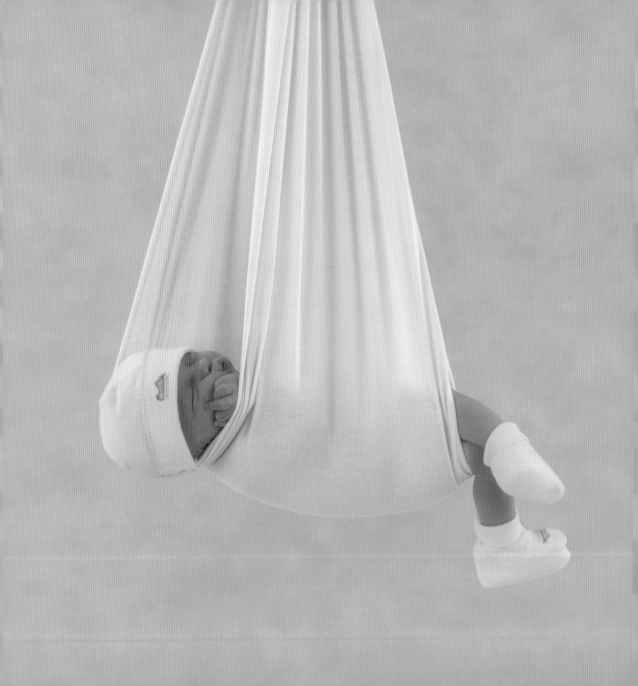

my birth

the date I was born

the time was

the place I was born

I was delivered by

I weighed

and measured

the people present were

photos

photos

mementos

ultrasound ~ birth announcement ~ hospital tag ~ a lock of hair ~ emails

mementos

gift cards ~ pressed flowers ~ birthday horoscope ~ newspaper clippings

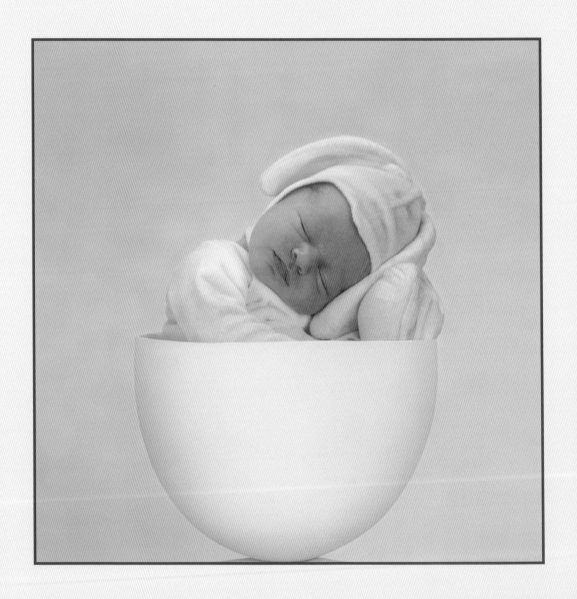

special messages

my first visitors

special messages and gifts I received

_____

_____

_____

_____

_____

_____

_____

_____

_____

_____

_____

_____

my homecoming

the date I came home
_____

_____

my address
_____

_____

_____

_____

how my family felt that day
_____

_____

_____

_____

_____

_____

_____

photos

my name

my full name is
_____

my name was chosen by
_____

my name means
_____
_____

my nicknames are
_____

ceremonies celebrating my birth
_____

the venue was
_____

comments
_____

my handprints

my footprints

my family tree

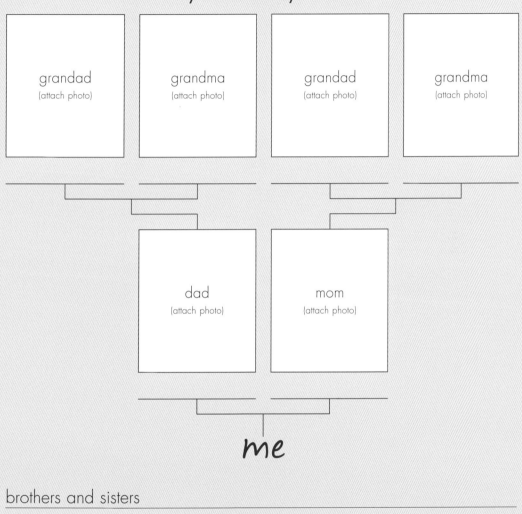

grandad
(attach photo)

grandma
(attach photo)

grandad
(attach photo)

grandma
(attach photo)

dad
(attach photo)

mom
(attach photo)

me

brothers and sisters

who I look like

my hair looks like
_____

_____

my skin looks like
_____

_____

my nose looks like
_____

_____

my eyes look like
_____

_____

my mouth looks like
_____

_____

my chin looks like
_____

_____

my cheeks look like
_____

_____

photos

three months

my weight _____ my length _____

what I'm like _____

_____

_____

_____

what makes me smile _____

_____

_____

_____

what I like doing _____

_____

_____

_____

_____

photos

six months

my weight _____ my length _____

what I'm like _____

_____

_____

_____

what I can do now _____

_____

_____

_____

what sounds I make _____

_____

_____

_____

_____

photos

nine months

my weight _____   my length _____

what I'm like _____

_____

_____

what makes me laugh _____

_____

_____

what I like doing _____

_____

_____

_____

_____

my first birthday

my weight _____ my height _____

my first words _____

_____

_____

what's happening in my world _____

_____

_____

my favorite toys _____

_____

_____

my favorite foods _____

_____

_____

my pets _____

_____

photos

my first birthday party

we celebrated my birthday at

_____

_____

who was there

_____

_____

_____

my presents were

_____

_____

_____

my first birthday cake was

_____

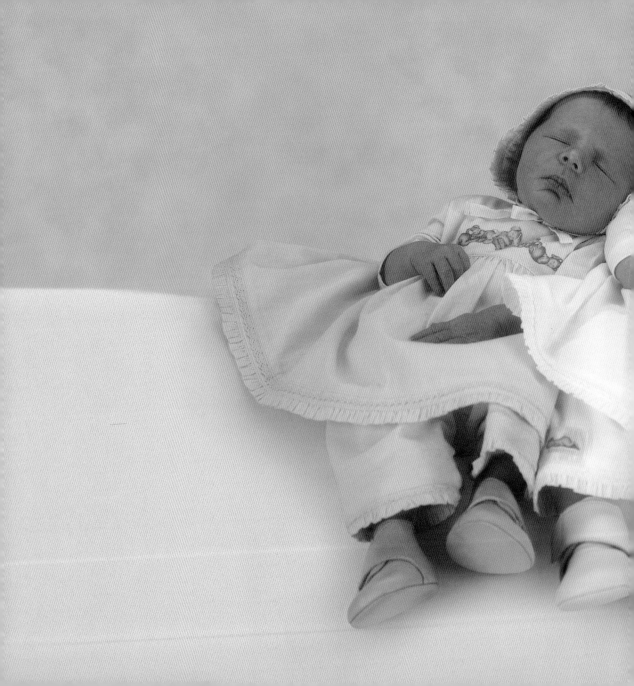

milestones

I first smiled

I first laughed

I first grasped a toy

I first slept through the night

I first held my head up

I first rolled over

I first sat up

I first crawled

I first stood up

I first walked

my first tooth

my first word

other milestones

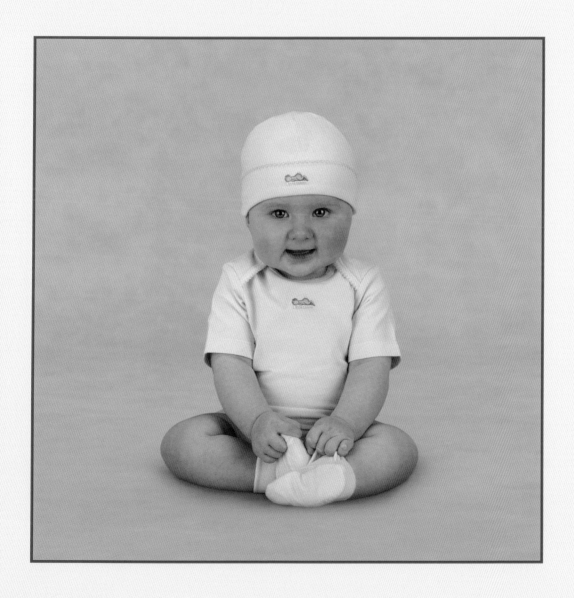

photos

my first holiday

where we went

_____

_____

_____

who was there

_____

_____

_____

what we did

_____

_____

_____

my favorite thing was

_____

_____

_____

my second birthday

my weight _____ my height _____

what I'm like _____

_____

_____

_____

some words I can say _____

_____

_____

_____

my favorite toys _____

_____

_____

my favorite books _____

_____

_____

my second birthday party

we celebrated my birthday at
_____
_____
_____

who was there
_____
_____
_____
_____

my presents were
_____
_____
_____
_____

my birthday cake was
_____
_____

photos

my favorite things

food

_____

_____

clothes

_____

_____

music

_____

_____

stories

_____

_____

animals

_____

_____

toys

_____

_____

activities

_____

_____

_____

my best friends

_____

_____

_____

photo

photo

_____

_____

_____

photos

_____

_____

_____

photo

photo

_____

_____

_____

ANNE GEDDES ®

www.annegeddes.com

© 2005 Anne Geddes

First published in 2005 by Photogenique Publishers
(a division of Hachette Livre NZ Ltd)
4 Whetu Place, Mairangi Bay, Auckland, New Zealand

This edition published in 2005 in North America,
United Kingdom, and Republic of Ireland by
Andrews McMeel Publishing,
an Andrews McMeel Universal company,
4520 Main Street, Kansas City, Missouri 64111

Produced by Kel Geddes
Printed in China by Midas Printing Limited, Hong Kong

ISBN-13: 978-0-7407-5602-3

ISBN-10: 0-7407-5602-8

www.andrewsmcmeel.com